GW00371623

SEIZE THE DAY

live in the moment

summersdale

SEIZE THE DAY

First published as *Carpe Diem* in 2013
This edition copyright © Summersdale Publishers Ltd, 2016

Summersdale Publishers Ltd
46 West Street
Chichester
West Sussex
PO19 1RP
UK

www.summersdale.com

Printed and bound in the Czech Republic

ISBN: 978-1-84953-909-8

Substantial discounts on bulk quantities of Summersdale books are available to corporations, professional associations and other organisations. For details contact Nicky Douglas by telephone: +44 (0) 1243 756902, fax: +44 (0) 1243 786300 or email: nicky@summersdale.com.

To..............................

From..........................

CARPE
DIEM

THE ENVIOUS MOMENT
IS FLYING NOW,
NOW, WHILE WE'RE SPEAKING:
SEIZE THE DAY.

Horace

OPEN THE CURTAINS AND LET A NEW DAY BEGIN!

Opportunities
multiply as they
are seized.

Sun Tzu

GOOD THINGS COME TO THOSE WHO...

...GO OUT
AND GET
THEM!

"

Act as if what
you do makes a
difference.
It does.

William James

With the
new day
comes new
strength and
NEW THOUGHTS.

Eleanor Roosevelt

BUILD SOMETHING TODAY, HOWEVER SMALL.

> I'd rather regret the things I've done than regret the things I haven't done.

LUCILLE BALL

If you're going through hell, keep going.

Winston Churchill

WITHOUT
OBSTACLES,
LIFE WOULD
JUST BE
A RACE -
AND THAT
WOULDN'T BE
HALF AS
MUCH FUN.

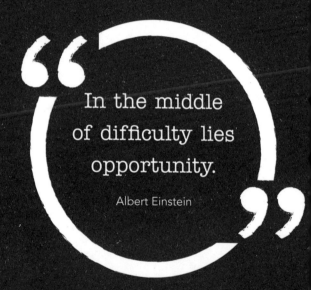

"
In the middle
of difficulty lies
opportunity.

Albert Einstein

One may walk over the
highest mountain one
step at a time.

John Wanamaker

YOU'RE
ONLY
CONFINED
BY THE
WALLS
YOU BUILD
YOURSELF.

" Things do not happen. Things are made to happen. "

John F. Kennedy

In order to
succeed, we
must first
BELIEVE
that we can.

Nikos Kazantzakis

TODAY IS A BLANK PAGE - WHAT ARE YOU GOING TO WRITE ON IT?

Opportunities are like sunrises – if you wait too long, you miss them.

William Arthur Ward

. . . .

If you ask me what I
came into this life to
do, I will tell you: I
came to live out loud.

Émile Zola

. . . .

BEING ALIVE IS A SPECIAL OCCASION.

> Do not follow where
> the path may lead.
> Go instead where
> there is no path
> and leave a trail.

Harold R. McAlindon

**Whenever you fall,
pick something up.**

Oswald Avery

EVERY
CHANGE
BRINGS
OPPORTUNITY
WITH IT.

I couldn't wait for
success, so I went
ahead without it.

Jonathan Winters

Tell me, what is
it you plan to do
with your one wild
and precious life?

Mary Oliver

LIFE BEGINS WHEN YOU DO.

Expect problems
and eat them
for breakfast.

Alfred A. Montapert

The most effective
way to do it,
is to do it.

Amelia Earhart

MAKE IT HAPPEN!

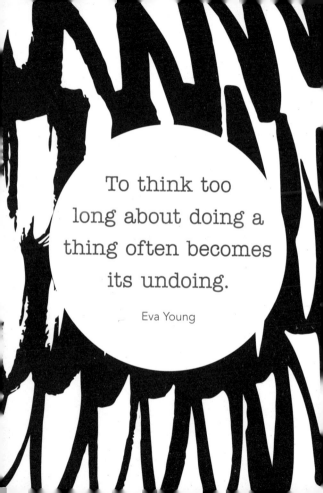

To think too
long about doing a
thing often becomes
its undoing.

Eva Young

To know oneself, one should assert oneself.

Albert Camus

LISTEN TO YOUR INNER VOICE.

"

Look at life through
the windshield, not
the rear-view mirror.

BYRD BAGGETT

"

No matter how you feel, get up, dress up and show up.

Regina Brett

YOU ARE THE HERO OF YOUR STORY.

With the past,
I have nothing to do;
nor with the future.
I live now.

Ralph Waldo Emerson

Nothing is
worth more
than this day.

Johann Wolfgang von Goethe

WHAT ARE YOU WAITING FOR?

Nothing really matters except what you do now in this instant of time.

Eileen Caddy

MAKE A
WISH...

KE

ISH

E

... THEN
MAKE IT
COME TRUE!

,,

I am an optimist.
It does not seem
too much use being
anything else.

Winston Churchill

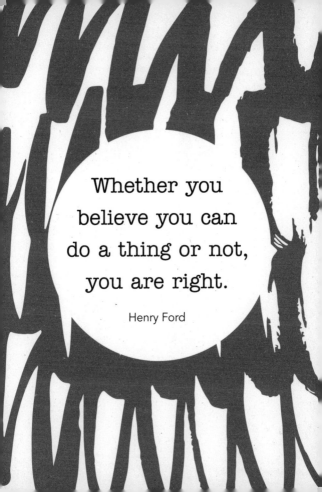

Whether you believe you can do a thing or not, you are right.

Henry Ford

WHO'S
THAT IN THE
MIRROR?
LOOKS LIKE
A GO-GETTER
TO ME.

• • • • • • • • • • • • • •

Life isn't about finding
yourself; it's about
creating yourself.

George Bernard Shaw

• • • • • • • • • • • • • •

Do what you can,
with what you've got,
where you are.

Bill Widener

WHEN LIFE THROWS TOMATOES AT YOU, MAKE A BLOODY MARY!

Don't live down
to expectations. Go
out there and do
something remarkable.

Wendy Wasserstein

"

If you can find
a path with no
obstacles,
it probably doesn't
lead anywhere.

Frank A. Clark

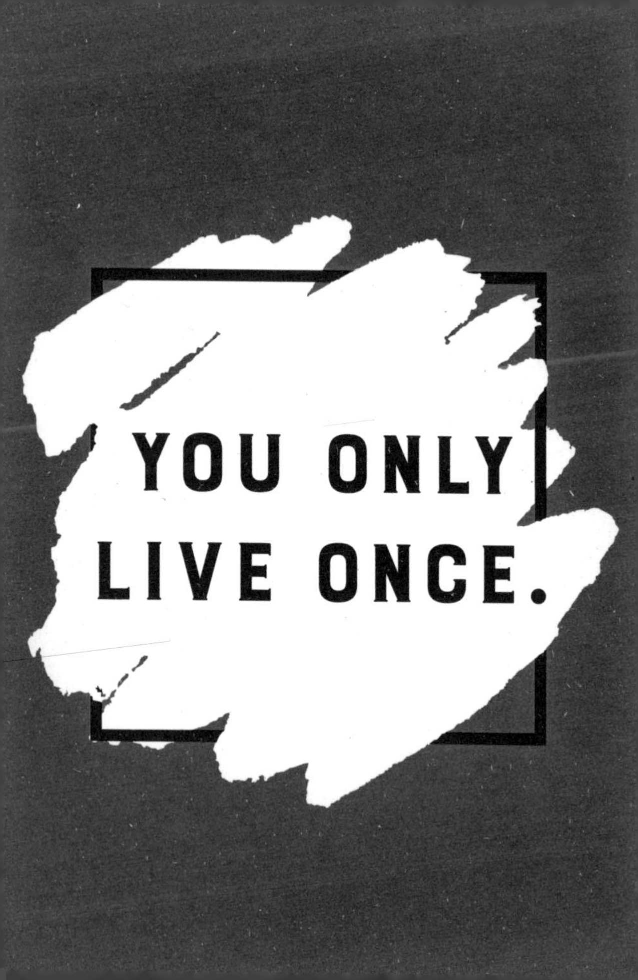
YOU ONLY
LIVE ONCE.

Opportunity does not knock, it presents itself when you beat down the door.

Kyle Chandler

Begin to be
now what you
will be hereafter.

William James

SQUEEZE ALL THE JUICE OUT OF TODAY!

"

Set your goals high,
and don't stop till
you get there.

Bo Jackson

Live as if you
were to die tomorrow.
Learn as if you were
to live forever.

Mahatma Gandhi

YOUR LIFE IS A WORK OF ART - IT DESERVES TO BE SEEN.

Find ecstasy in life;
the mere sense of
living is joy enough.

Emily Dickinson

No one
knows what
he can do
TILL HE TRIES.

Publilius Syrus

DON'T
RACE FOR
THE FINISH
LINE -
ENJOY THE
JOURNEY.

If you wait, all that
happens is that you
get older.

Mario Andretti

The word 'now' is like a bomb thrown through the window, and it ticks.

Arthur Miller

MAKE EVERY MINUTE COUNT.

"

It's always too
early to quit.

NORMAN VINCENT PEALE

"

It's all right to have butterflies in your stomach. Just get them to fly in formation.

Rob Gilbert

GRAB A DOUBLE HELPING OF LIFE, WITH A SIDE ORDER OF ADVENTURE.

"

Life is either a
daring adventure,
or nothing.

Helen Keller

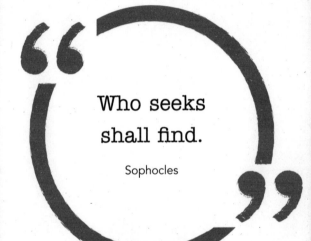

"

Who seeks
shall find.

Sophocles

LIFE IS OFTEN SWEET, SOMETIMES SOUR, BUT ALWAYS WORTH TASTING.

There are always
flowers for those who
want to see them.

Henri Matisse

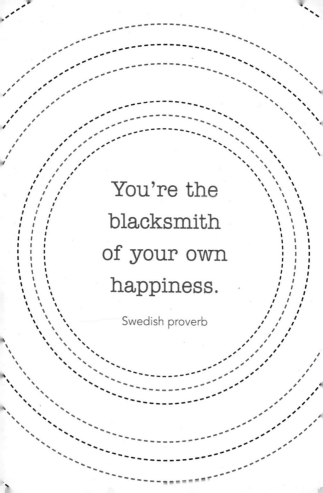

You're the blacksmith of your own happiness.

Swedish proverb

TO REST IS TO RUST. STAY SHINY AND BRIGHT!

Every artist was first an amateur.

Ralph Waldo Emerson

Some days there won't be a song in your heart. Sing anyway.

Emory Austin

EVERY DAWN IS A NEW BEGINNING, A TIME TO START A NEW STORY.

. . . .

Don't loaf and invite
inspiration; light out
after it with a club.

Jack London

. . . .

Never put off
till tomorrow
what may be done
the day after tomorrow
JUST AS WELL.

Mark Twain

SING A SONG, PAINT A PICTURE... CHANGE THE WORLD.

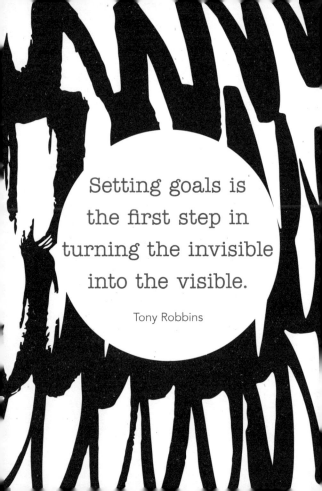

Setting goals is
the first step in
turning the invisible
into the visible.

Tony Robbins

"

The wise man does
at once what the
fool does finally.

BALTASAR GRACIÁN

"

REAL LIFE IS MORE EXCITING THAN ANYTHING ON A SCREEN - LIVE IT!

You can't
use up creativity.
The more you use,
the more you have.

Maya Angelou

Live today,
for tomorrow it
will all be history.

Proverb

GO THE EXTRA MILE; IT'S NEVER CROWDED.

Do it and
then you will feel
motivated to do it.

Zig Ziglar

Live the questions now. Perhaps you will then gradually, without noticing it, live along some distant day into the answer.

Rainer Maria Rilke

LIVE YOUR DREAMS.

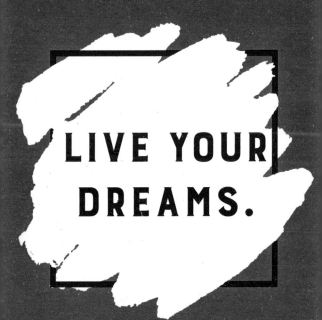

• • • • • • • • • • • • •

It is never too
late to be what you
might have been.

Adelaide Anne Procter

• • • • • • • • • • • • • •

We are all in
the gutter, but
some of us are
looking at the stars.

Oscar Wilde

LIVE LIFE
OFF THE
MAP AND
BE YOUR
OWN
COMPASS.

"

The best way to
predict the future is
to create it.

Peter Drucker

A journey of
a thousand miles
begins with a
SINGLE STEP.

Lao Tzu

TALK TO SOMEONE NEW. YOU COULD MAKE THEIR DAY - AND THEY MIGHT MAKE YOURS.

Seize the moment.
Man was never intended
to become an oyster.

Theodore Roosevelt

YOU ARE
A SONG...

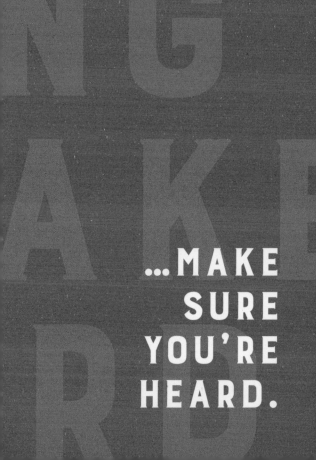

...MAKE
SURE
YOU'RE
HEARD.

"

Life shrinks or
expands according
to one's courage.

ANAÏS NIN

"

The best way
to make your
dreams come true
is to wake up.

Paul Valéry

LOOK AT
LIFE FROM
UNEXPECTED
ANGLES
TODAY.

· · · · · · · · · · · · · · ·

Go for it now. The
future is promised
to no one.

Wayne Dyer

· · · · · · · · · · · · · · ·

Tomorrow is
often the busiest
day of the week.

Spanish proverb

BE WHO YOU'VE ALWAYS WANTED TO BE.

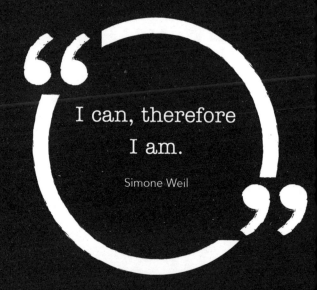

"
I can, therefore
I am.

Simone Weil
"

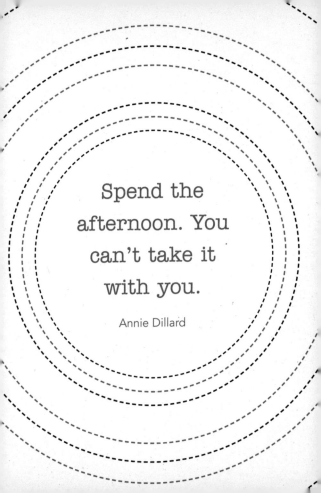

Spend the
afternoon. You
can't take it
with you.

Annie Dillard

MAKE YOUR OWN SUNSHINE.

Look at
everything always
as though you were
seeing it either
for the first or
LAST TIME.

Betty Smith

The man who removes a mountain begins by carrying away small stones.

Chinese proverb

YOU CAN DO IT. ALL YOU HAVE TO DO IS TRY.

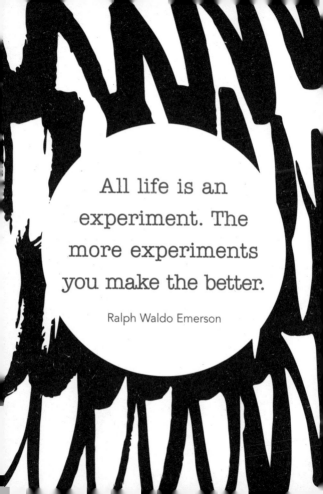

All life is an experiment. The more experiments you make the better.

Ralph Waldo Emerson

"

If your ship
doesn't come in,
swim out to it.

JONATHAN WINTERS

"

JUST BE
YOURSELF.

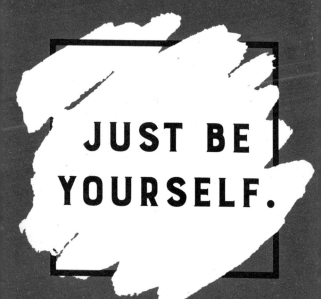

Life begins at
the end of your
comfort zone.

Neale Donald Walsch

• • • • • • • • • • • •

There are exactly as
many special occasions
in life as we choose
to celebrate.

Robert Brault

• • • • • • • • • • • •

LIFE IS NOT A REHEARSAL. ENJOY THE LIMELIGHT!

To me, every hour
of the light and
dark is a miracle.

Walt Whitman

If not now, when?

when?

Hillel the Elder

GO AND GET IT!

This very moment is a seed from which the flowers of tomorrow's happiness grow.

Margaret Lindsey

"

Either you run
the day or the day
runs you.

Jim Rohn

ENJOY
TODAY,
DON'T
WORRY
ABOUT
TOMORROW.

> " You can have
> anything you want
> if you are willing to
> give up the belief that
> you can't have it. "
>
> ROBERT ANTHONY

It's never too late – never too late to start over, never too late to be happy.

Jane Fonda

NOBODY CAN HOLD YOU BACK.

. . . .

You can't expect to
hit the jackpot if you
don't put a few nickels
in the machine.

Flip Wilson

. . . .

Change your life
today. Don't gamble
on the future, act now,
WITHOUT DELAY.

Simone de Beauvoir

SHOW THE WORLD WHAT YOU'RE MADE OF.

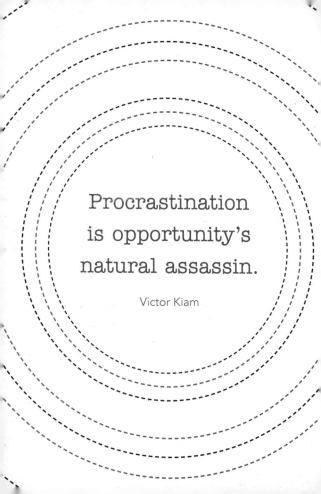

Procrastination
is opportunity's
natural assassin.

Victor Kiam

Shoot for the moon.
Even if you miss,
you'll land among
the stars.

Norman Vincent Peale

DRESS TO IMPRESS AND BE THE BEST YOU CAN BE.

Yesterday is gone.
Tomorrow has not yet
come. We have only
today. Let us begin.

Mother Teresa

To change one's life,
start immediately,
do it flamboyantly,
no exceptions.

William James

DON'T PUT OFF YOUR HAPPINESS.

Opportunity is missed
by most people because
it is dressed in overalls
and looks like work.

Anonymous

Difficulties strengthen the mind, as labour does the body.

Seneca

TURN YOUR HOPES INTO REALITIES.

> "Our greatest glory
> is not in never
> falling, but in rising
> every time we fall.

OLIVER GOLDSMITH

First say to yourself
what you would be;
and then do what
you have to do.

Epictetus

MAKE AN IMPRESSION!

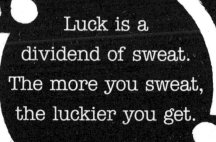

Luck is a dividend of sweat. The more you sweat, the luckier you get.

Ray Kroc

We are the ones we've been waiting for. We are the change that we seek.

Barack Obama

WELCOME
TODAY'S
CHALLENGES.

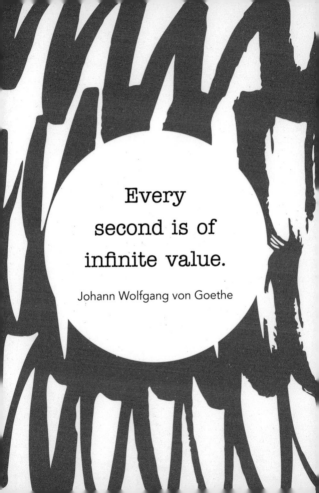

Every
second is of
infinite value.

Johann Wolfgang von Goethe

*The purpose of life
is to be happy.*

Dalai Lama

SPOT THE FLOWERS THAT GROW UP THROUGH THE CRACKS.

If the wind
will not serve,
take to the oars.

Latin proverb

"

May you live all the
days of your life.

Jonathan Swift

DOORS ARE
MADE TO
BE OPENED...

...LOCKS ARE
MADE TO
FIT A KEY.

The season of failure
is the best time for
sowing the seeds
of success.

Paramahansa Yogananda

Each day comes
bearing its own gifts.
Untie the ribbons.

Ruth Ann Schabacker

BE A GIFT TO THE WORLD TODAY.

A person who's
happy will make
others happy.

Anne Frank

MAKE NEW
CONNECTIONS
TODAY!

"

A mind is
like a parachute.
It doesn't work
if it's not open.

Frank Zappa

"

What matters is
to live in the present,
live now, for every
moment is now.

Sai Baba

WHEN'S THE BEST TIME TO START? NOW!

If you're interested in finding
out more about our books,
find us on Facebook at
Summersdale Publishers
and follow us on Twitter at
@Summersdale.